Lois Wyse, the grandmother of nine,
is the author of
Funny, You Don't Look Like a Grandmother,
Grandchildren Are So Much Fun,
I Should Have Had Them First,
and
Grandmother's Treasures.

For all grandmothers who through love,
devotion, and care help families achieve
and remember the best in life
and for
L. M. G.
because a sweet spirit never dies

Published by Crown Publishers, Inc., 201 East 50th Street,
New York, New York 10022. Member of the Crown Publishing Group.

Random House, Inc. New York, Toronto, London, Sydney, Auckland

CROWN is a trademark of Crown Publishers, Inc.

Manufactured in Singapore

ISBN 0-517-59699-7

10 9 8 7 6 5 4 3 2 1

First Edition

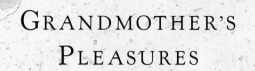

Grandmother's Pleasures

A Picture Memory Book

Conceived and written by
LOIS WYSE

Illustrated by
Judith Sutton

CROWN PUBLISHERS, INC.
NEW YORK

DEAR GRANDMOTHER,

Most of us keep our life in boxes. Sometimes they are shoe boxes stuffed with old photographs. Sometimes they are pretty boxes, beribboned and fussy—and stuffed with old photographs.

The purpose of this book is to help you edit your life, go through those old pictures, and find the best of your photographed memories, put them in this book and then share the stories of those pictures with your family. Of course, if you have a family that collects, they just may have the photographs at hand and assemble the book for you.

But no matter who does it, this is the book that is meant to take your life out of the hidden boxes and put it into the hands of those you love.

Your family deserves to have a collection and catalog of your life so they can understand how they came to be.

And then, if the book is really assembled as a document of pleasures, on days when the sky is dark and life is difficult, you can reach out to the past and from the strengths of your joys recall something that will give you—as well as your children and grandchildren—the fortitude to face the future.

LOIS WYSE

DEAR FAMILY,

*T*his is a book that pictures the best of my life and the best of our times.

Some of these memories are about you— and some are about people you may not have known. Still, they all have given me some of life's pleasures, and I share them with you for the enjoyment and understanding that they will hopefully give you.

_____

Your Grandmother

_____

Date

In gratitude for love given me,
I choose to give my love to thee.

THE PLEASURES OF FAMILY

❀

*Pictures of Those Who
Came Before Me*

THE PLEASURES
OF MARRIAGE

Events define our history of love.

THE PLEASURES OF BABIES...

❀

AND CHILDREN

Children and grandchildren are the dots
That connect the generations.

DATES TO REMEMBER

Birthdays and Anniversaries

THE PLEASURE OF
BIRTHDAYS

Birthdays are the benchmark
In our history of love.

THE PLEASURE OF
HOLIDAYS

The shortest route to renewal
Is through remembrance,
Remembrance of the times
That made us family.

THE PLEASURE OF
THEIR COMPANY

Faces and Places

All the understanding a woman needs
Is in the faces
Of those she loves.

THE SIMPLE PLEASURES

❀

A Gathering of Friends

Love is not a simple thing—
But only in the convoluted complexity of love
Do we find what we want most:
Faith, contentment, hope.

MILESTONES

The Turning Points
in Life

Look and recall,
For only through
Recollection
Do we become
The proud possessors
Of this collection.

SOME THINGS
I WILL
NEVER FORGET

Pictures and words are the
Working tools of memory.

MY FAVORITE PICTURE

Time goes by so fast,
But memory is forever.

In the heart
Live the dreams
The eyes do not
Always see.

So open your heart,
And your eyes will see
The love that is
Always there.